Speeches

"Speeches"

what to say at weddings
and when to say it

from confetti.co.uk
don't get married without us...

First published in 2001
by Octopus Publishing Group,
2–4 Heron Quays,
London E14 4JP
www.conran-octopus.co.uk
Reprinted in 2002, 2003 (twice)
Text copyright © 2001 Confetti Network
Book design and layout copyright
© 2001 Conran Octopus Limited
Illustrations copyright © Confetti Network

Publishing Director Lorraine Dickey
Senior Editor Katey Day
Copy-editor Helen Ridge
Creative Director Leslie Harrington
Designer Megan Smith
Jacket Designer Jo Raynsford
Production Director Zoë Fawcett

Thanks also to the staff at Confetti.co.uk,
brides, grooms, guests and Aunt Betti

ISBN 1 84091 224 3
Printed by Scotprint in Great Britain

Other books in this series include *The Wedding Planner*;
How to Write a Wedding Speech; *Confettiquette*; *Men at Weddings*;
Wedding Readings and Vows and *Wedding Readings*.

Contents

Few people are practised in the art of public speaking, so the thought of standing up in front of everyone at a wedding reception and sounding good is pretty intimidating. But don't panic. We have all the advice you need for preparing and making your speech.

Who speaks and when

Traditionally, the toastmaster or master of ceremonies will introduce the speeches at the end of the meal. The formal order of speakers is:

- Father of the bride (or a close family friend)
- The groom
- The best man

But if the bride, chief bridesmaid or guests want to speak, that's great, too!

Traditionally, the speeches take place after the meal, but some couples decide to have them beforehand to allow the speakers to enjoy their meal free of nerves.

The basics

- Firstly, don't panic. A little careful planning will help you deliver a speech that you'll be proud of.
- If you can, visit the reception venue to get an idea of where you'll be standing and the size of the room.
- You will need to project your voice, so practise speaking out loud.
- Find out if you are expected to say a few words and then propose a toast, or make a long speech.

- Is the reception going to have a theme that you could refer to in your speech or even incorporate into it?
- Are you responsible for presenting gifts to members of the wedding party?
- Find out a little about the guests and if there are any subjects you should avoid.
- How many guests will there be? As a general rule, the more people present, the more formal the speech.

Who says what

Here is a brief outline of who says what. For more details and for sample speeches, turn to the relevant chapters.

Father of the bride or friend of the family

- Thanks the guests for coming and participating in the special day.
- Thanks everyone who has contributed to the cost of the wedding.
- Compliments and praises the bride, and welcomes her new husband into the family.
- Toasts the bride and groom.

Bridegroom

- Thanks the father of the bride for his toast.
- Thanks the guests for attending and for their gifts.
- Thanks both sets of parents.
- Compliments his bride.
- Thanks his best man.
- Thanks and toasts the bridesmaids.

Best man

- Thanks the groom for his toast to the bridesmaids.
- Comments on the bridal couple, particularly the groom.
- Reads any messages from absent friends and relatives.
- Toasts the bride and groom.

Bride

- Thanks the guests for coming.
- Thanks her parents and bridesmaids.
- Compliments the groom.
- Proposes a toast.

Chief bridesmaid

- Thanks the bride.
- Compliments the ushers.
- Proposes a toast.

Planning your speech

- First, decide whether you want to write out your speech and read it word for word, or memorize it completely, or simply compile a list of bullet points to prompt you.
- Start by noting suitable headings to focus on, then fill in the spaces to produce an entire speech.
- All wedding speeches are just extended toasts, so don't worry that yours has to be worthy of an Oscar winner.
- Make your speech relevant to all the guests, some of whom may not know the bride and groom very well.
- Keep your speech quite brief – around five minutes is a good average.

On the big day

- Try not to let the speech dominate your thoughts and stop you enjoying the occasion.
- Avoid too much alcohol before your speech, as it may cloud your judgement. This is especially true if you find a drink or two slurs your speech.
- If you're concerned that your voice will not carry very well, ask one of the ushers or a member of the venue staff to stand at the back of the room when you start your speech and indicate if they can't hear you.
- When it's your turn to speak, don't get up until you have been introduced. The guests are likely to applaud you, and this creates a welcome distraction while you stand and clear your throat. Begin your speech by taking a deep breath and smiling, if at all possible!
- Adrenaline will carry you to the end of your speech before you know it. If you make a mistake, smile, correct yourself and continue.
- Remember to speak slowly – if you're nervous, you're likely to gabble. If you feel yourself racing away, stop, take a deep breath and then continue.
- Try to enjoy yourself as you make your speech and think of the meaning behind your words, so that everyone is clear of your feelings for those you're speaking about.
- At the end of your speech you are likely to be proposing a toast. Invite your guests to stand to drink the toast, then sit as they sit, after the toast.
- Having done all of this, relax and enjoy the applause, and the rest of the day!

20 top tips

Take note

As soon as you know that you'll be making a speech at the wedding – this is usually some time in advance – get into the habit of carrying a notebook around with you so you can jot down any thoughts or memories that could be worked into your speech. The best ideas often come to you at the most unlikely moments...

Structure your speech

Don't try writing it all in one go! Break down your words into the different areas you want to cover, such as thanking the guests, stories about the run-up to the wedding, anecdotes about the groom, words for the bride and your speech's conclusion. Take the jottings from your notebook and see where they fit into the plan.

Get sorted – in triplicate

Anxiety about losing the text of your speech can ruin a whole wedding morning. Make three or four copies of the final version and give each one to separate guests to look after. It's impossible for all the copies to be lost – and it will put your mind at rest!

Make eye contact

… but not with everyone at once! Speak as if you were talking to one person, and address them directly. Of course, you will want to look around the room, but take time to focus on one person at a time.

Everyone's rooting for you!

It's true. This is a wedding and, although the scale of the occasion might initially seem daunting, it is in many ways the easiest public speaking opportunity of all. Everyone is on your side and no one wants you to do badly.

Practise – on tape

Reading your speech out again and again – preferably to other people – is essential when you're practising. Making a recording of yourself can be useful, too. Listen out for places where you speak too fast or where the point you're making is unclear, and revise your speech accordingly.

Speak to both sides

Make sure your speech will mean something to everyone present. There may be guests who know only half of the wedding party (if that), and they may not even know you. In-jokes and favourite anecdotes should be told in such a way that everyone can enjoy them, so explain any esoteric references as you go.

Don't rely on memory

You may have practised your speech so hard that you're sure you know it by heart. Keep your text handy anyway – the stress of public speaking can sometimes cause people to forget their lines.

Be brief

Brevity truly is the soul of wit. Some speakers plan optional sections that can be cut if the speech isn't going too well. At any rate, you should time your speech and stick to it – five minutes is perfectly long enough.

But they didn't laugh...

Keep jokes and anecdotes short, so that if one doesn't work, you can swiftly move on to the next. And don't laugh at your own jokes – you'll soon know whether you've scored a hit!

Get your stories straight

Often a bride and groom may have a story in their past that lends itself to a good anecdote. But if the story is at all well known, check with the other speakers just to make sure that your material doesn't duplicate anyone else's.

Language barrier

Although to you your speech is something written, to your guests it is something spoken. So make sure your language is not too stiff or formal. Change all the 'could nots' to 'couldn'ts', and make free with the first person!

It's not a speech...

In most people's minds, the word 'speech' is associated with great tension, formality and the need to perform well. But thinking of it instead as part of a conversation at a largish dinner party, or simply as a few words to wish some friends well, will make the whole thing seem less intimidating.

Playing the waiting game

Actually sitting and waiting for your moment to come is probably more stressful than the speaking itself. Once you're up and away, the momentum of the speech takes over and you'll start to relax once you hear a laugh or two. So, while you're waiting, repeat your first line to yourself. It also helps if you can get involved in the other speeches – really make a point of listening and responding to them. It'll be your turn before you know it.

It's your call

There are traditions and customs about who should speak and what they should say but, if it suits you, feel free to ignore any or all of them. Give the speech on your own terms and you'll achieve the best result. So, if you want to give only a brief toast rather than a long spiel, fine. If you're the best man and you don't feel like humiliating the groom, that's fine, too. It's entirely up to you.

Breathing space

When speaking or reading in public, people have a marked tendency to rush their words without realizing it. So, it's a good idea to insert the word 'pause' at intervals in your speech or, if you're using cue cards, to insert blank cards that will automatically slow you down.

Doing the introductions

If you have a toastmaster, he or she should take care of introducing each speaker. Otherwise, this is the best man's job. Make sure that each speaker is introduced by name and position before they start – this will stop guests talking among themselves as they try to work out who's speaking.

Not now...

Whenever the speeches are scheduled to take place – at the end of the meal is the norm – make sure that nothing else is going on and that all the clearing up has stopped. Speakers need everyone's undivided attention!

Preparing the speech

When writing your speech, always bear in mind at what point your speech comes in the order of play. Will you need to cover certain subjects? Will you be speaking on behalf of anyone? Will you be expected to address certain themes? Will you need to reply to another speaker/toast? These considerations should help you plan your words.

Full stop

However silly or serious your speech may be, it's always a good idea to end it with a toast. For you, it's something to work towards and, for the guests, it's an immediately recognizable punctuation point.

For more information, advice and sample speeches, visit the speech centre at confetti.co.uk/speeches/p15

The father of the bride's speech

Welcome to the weird and wonderful world of weddings. Your daughter has chosen to marry, and it is your duty to send her into married life by celebrating her pre-wedding years in a sentimental – and possibly amusing – way. You've waited all your life for this crucial moment, so take the time to enjoy it. This is your chance to tell her how much you care for her and let everyone else know how wonderful she is. Make the most of it.

Traditionally, the father of the bride is the first speaker (apart from a brief introduction from the best man), so your speech is a sort of scene-setter. The idea behind this is doubtless linked to the fact that the father of the bride was always supposed to foot the bill for the wedding – so, if you're paying, you should at least be allowed to get your oar in first! Even today, fathers of brides are often advised to begin with a 'gesture of humility', thanking anyone else who has contributed to the cost of the wedding.

In your speech, you'll probably want to talk about your daughter as – again, as tradition would have it – you hand her over from your care into that of her new husband. Father and daughter have a special relationship, but try to avoid the clichés and talk realistically and affectionately about your own specific relationship: its ups and downs, the funny foibles and the silly stories.

Your speech also allows you to officially welcome the groom into your family, so you may want to talk about how you first got to know him. You might also want to mention the joining together of your family and the groom's, the happy times the two families have already shared and/or say how you look forward to the prospect of getting to know each other better.

Of course, your remarks will be made on your partner's behalf as well (unless she is also going to make a speech). If your partner has died, this may be the moment to say a few words in her memory.

The basics

So what do you have to say?

- Thank the guests for coming to the wedding and being involved in such a special day. Remember to mention anyone who has travelled a long distance.
- Thank anyone who has made some kind of financial contribution to the wedding.
- Tell your daughter how proud you are of her.
- Welcome your new son-in-law into your family.
- Reminisce about your daughter's pre-wedding years.
- Wish the newlyweds success and happiness in the future.
- Propose a toast to the bride and groom.

The father of the bride's speech is generally expected to be the least funny and often the most sentimental, which should make the job of writing it the easiest. But it's not always the case. This speech is often the one that has been anticipated for the longest period of time and is probably if not the most emotional, then certainly the one filled with the most pride. The father of the bride begins the speeches, thus setting the tone for the rest of the proceedings. The best advice is to stay mostly with convention, unless you're feeling particularly brave or imaginative. It's easier to write a speech starting with the traditional component parts: welcoming the guests, thanking everyone, talking about the bride, welcoming the groom and, finally, the toast. If you'd like to inject some humour, turn to page 27 for advice.

If you know what you'd like to say, but aren't sure how to say it, here are some suggestions with some options to consider incorporating into your speech.

1. The welcome

- Thank you all for coming and sharing this special day with Nicola and John.
- I'd like to take this opportunity to thank you all for being here. I know that some of you have had further to come than others, but you are all welcome guests on this happy *day/night*.
- Ladies and gentlemen, I'm delighted to see so many of you here today to celebrate the marriage of my daughter Nicola to John.

2. The thanks

- Nicola and John have worked very hard to pay for today, and it's been worth it. This is a lovely *meal/reception*, and everything looks perfect. I'm proud of the pair of you.
- Weddings are not cheap occasions, but my *little girl/ daughter* deserves the best and, as you can see, she's got it. This would not have been possible without the generous help of John's parents, George and Amy.
- This wedding has taken a lot of time and patience to organize, and decisions have sometimes been difficult to reach *[make a small joke about the struggle it was to decide between a sophisticated colour scheme or an outrageous one of pink with yellow spots]*, but I'm really delighted that everything's turned out so well. In particular, I'd like to thank the *florist/minister/ bridesmaids* for the amount of trouble they have gone to. *Everything/the church/the hall/the hotel/the bouquet looks/look* wonderful.

3. The bride

- I have always known that Nicola is a beautiful woman, but I have never seen her look quite so beautiful or so radiant as she does today. I'm extremely proud of her.
- Nicola has had many roles in life... (for example, daughter, fiancée, student, air hostess, etc.) but never has she looked more beautiful than as a bride.
- When Nicola told me that she was going to get married, I was worried that she wouldn't be my little girl any more but, seeing her today as a beautiful bride, I realize that, no matter how old she is, she will always be my little girl, and I love her.
- This *elegant/beautiful/radiant/lovely* bride is a far cry from the Nicola I remember so well, who was always in trouble for being *messy/muddy/late/a tomboy/scruffy*, but, no matter what she looks like, I love her and am very proud to be her father.

If you're not the bride's father, there are many ways to convey how proud you are to take on this role.

- I am not Nicola's father but I know that he would have been so proud of her today, as I am.
- Nicola has been my comfort and joy, and I am honoured that she chose me to give this speech.
- As Nicola's brother, I am supposed to be nasty to her and pull her hair to remind her that I am older than she is. Trouble is, she looks too gorgeous today. Still, I am very proud to be giving her away on behalf of our family. John, please look after her!

4. Welcome the groom

Here are a few ideas with a number of options to cut and paste into your own speech.

- There are not many men good enough for Nicola, but John is. When she turned up with a *scruffy/spotty/runny-nosed/well-groomed/lanky/large/tall/pony-tailed* man, I was *suspicious/delighted/dismayed/curious/welcoming*, *and/but* I *never hoped/really hoped* that they would marry. *And/But* they have, and I am really pleased for them. John is a *good/delightful/fun/great/lovely* man, and they make a wonderful couple.
- John is one of that rare breed of men – he really is as *good/sincere/wonderful/perfect/much of a creep* as he appears, and I am absolutely delighted to welcome him into *our/my family*.
- Nicola always claimed that she would never *get married/find the right man/love anyone/be happy,* but she was wrong. In John she has found the perfect partner, and I am delighted he has become a part of *my/our* family.
- What can I say about John? He is a *great/perfect/lovely/wonderful/good* man, and no one else would be as perfect for *my daughter/Nicola*. I'm delighted that he's decided to become part of the family.

5. General chat

This is your chance to make a few gentle jokes, but nothing crude or offensive. You might even want to quote something or recite a poem.

- Marriage, as I know all too well, is about compromise and, to keep things running smoothly, it's good to talk. However, as Helen Rowland said, 'Before marriage, a man will lie awake thinking about something you said; after marriage, he'll fall asleep before you finish saying it.'
- The best guarantee for a peaceful marriage is simple – lie. If she asks you if you've done whatever you've forgotten to do, say that you have and then do it. If he catches you doing something you shouldn't, say you did it as a surprise for him. Men are stupid; they'll believe anything, or at least pretend to, for a peaceful life!

- Nicola always said that she'd never find that special someone, but I'm delighted to see that she has. I just want to read something now because it seems so appropriate and expresses exactly what I mean. It's called *Destiny* and is by Sir Edwin Arnold:

  Somewhere there waiteth in this world of ours
  For one lone soul another lonely soul,
  Each choosing each through all the weary hours
  And meeting strangely at one sudden goal.
  Then blend they, like green leaves with golden flowers,
  Into one beautiful and perfect whole;
  And life's long night is ended, and the way
  Lies open onward to eternal day.

- You may think that this wedding has cost a lot but, as Goethe said, 'The sum which two married people owe to one another defies calculation. It is an infinite debt, which can only be discharged through all eternity.' I wonder if their bank manager would believe that?
- As a certain German philosopher once said: 'To marry is to halve your rights and double your duties', but if that were all there is to it, then none of us would get married in the first place. I'm delighted that Nicola and John have taken the plunge, otherwise none of us would be here enjoying this fine **champagne/wine/beer/tap water**.

6. The toast

By the time you get to the toast, it's almost time for you to sit down – but not quite. Finish with a flourish and then relax – the rest of the day/evening/night is yours to enjoy!

- Ladies and gentlemen, please be upstanding. I give you... the bride and groom.
- Ladies and gentlemen, please charge your glasses. I give you... the bride and groom.
- Honoured guests, please join me in the traditional toast. I give you... the bride and groom.
- Ladies and gentlemen, please be upstanding and raise your glasses. I give you... the bride and groom.

For more information about the father of the bride's role and duties, go to www.confetti.co.uk/speeches/p26

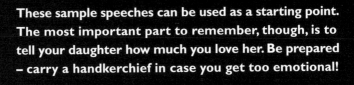

These sample speeches can be used as a starting point. The most important part to remember, though, is to tell your daughter how much you love her. Be prepared – carry a handkerchief in case you get too emotional!

SAMPLE SPEECH: A touch of humour

This is an important day for me. It's certainly not the time for jokes but the time when I resuscitate my bank account and hand over Sarah's spending habits to someone else.

The good thing about weddings is that you can show everyone how generous you are. I wanted to give you all an itemized bill so that you could see for yourselves how much these flowers cost, but Angela told me that it was not the done thing... as she slipped on her £150 hat!

Seriously, I have looked forward to this day for years. Sarah makes a stunning bride and John is a good man, and I wish them every happiness for the future. If they are any bit as happy as my wife and I, then they will be very happy indeed.

Marriage is an important commitment, so much so that you need a mortgage to pay for it! But it takes more than that. It needs patience and compromise, and I should know – I've been patiently compromising for years!

Bob's just looked at his watch, which is the signal that he needs a drink, so, ladies and gentlemen, please be upstanding. I give you... the bride and groom.

SAMPLE SPEECH: **Short and sweet**

When Sarah was a little girl, she used to lift her dress over her head and pretend it was a veil. Fortunately, she's acquired a bit more finesse since then, and today she is the most beautiful bride I have seen since I married her mother more than 30 years ago. I am so proud that my little girl has grown into such a beautiful and accomplished woman.

This wedding has been a huge family affair and today we become one big family. I'd like to thank John's parents, on behalf of the bride and groom, for their generosity. Without it we would not all be sitting down to such a lovely meal in such a beautiful hotel, and I'm grateful to them for helping to make this day so special for my youngest daughter.

What can I say about John? Quite simply, Sarah couldn't have chosen better. He's everything I would have looked for in a son-in-law and I'm delighted that he's joining our family.

I don't want to bore you with how happy I am today, so I'll finish up with the traditional toast said from the heart. Ladies and gentleman, I give you… the bride and groom.

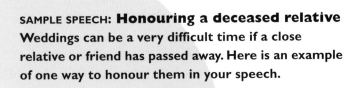

SAMPLE SPEECH: Honouring a deceased relative
Weddings can be a very difficult time if a close relative or friend has passed away. Here is an example of one way to honour them in your speech.

Standing here in front of all of you today, I feel incredibly old. To me, it was only yesterday that Sarah was born, and I never thought that I'd ever be as happy as I was then, but I was wrong. Seeing my daughter look as radiant as she does on her wedding day makes me happier than I ever thought possible. I am so proud of everything that she has become. My only regret is that her mother, Angela, cannot be with us. But this is not a day for regrets – it is a day for happiness and looking ahead.

I am so pleased that Sarah and John found each other. I never thought that anyone would be good enough for my little girl, but I am delighted to be proved wrong. John is a lovely man who makes my daughter happy. What more could I ask?

I don't want to delay the proceedings any longer with my memories of Sarah growing up, like the time when she was almost expelled for trying to burn down her school so she could have a day off – she never was very practical! Instead, I am going to ask you all to be upstanding and join me in a toast. Ladies and gentlemen, please raise your glasses. I give you… the bride and groom.

SAMPLE SPEECH: **Straight and sentimental**

I'm so pleased you could all be here on this wonderful occasion, which Lisa and David have gone to so much trouble to make absolutely perfect. It's a wonderful start to their married life together, which I know we all hope will be as successful as today is proving to be.

Success in marriage is more than finding the right person – it is being the right person – and I am proud to be here celebrating the marriage of these two lovely people, who are not only amazing in their own right, but are also the right people for each other.

Lisa, over the past ten months when you've been planning this wedding, your mother and I have had plenty of opportunities to observe you demonstrating all those fantastic qualities you have possessed since you were a girl. You have been creative in your planning, patient when things went wrong, generous and helpful to others, intelligent when dealing with difficult situations and a delight to be with. You remind me of your mother.

In short, Lisa has been everything you could want in a daughter, and I can only wish that she and David will be as happy as Mary and I have been during the last 34 years.

Ladies and gentlemen, please charge your glasses and join me in a toast. I give you. the bride and groom!

SAMPLE SPEECH: **Brief and witty**

Let me just start saying that I'm delighted to see so many of you here today. There's lots of people I recognize, a few of them looking far more grown up and elegant than usual, I'm talking mainly of course about my children here, and I hope to meet many more of you before the evening ends.

Well I'm going to keep this brief, because [looking at glass] Claire has made me pay for this, and while I'm up here and you're down there, I can't be doing my fair share of drinking! However, Claire has assured me she won't be imbibing too much of the potent stuff today, which I have to say was a relief, to both myself and my bank manager.

This isn't of course the first time my bank manager and I have spoken about keeping Claire in the manner to which she'd like to become accustomed – I seem to remember the pony, tennis camp, was it ballet lessons? Naturally I always said no, because I was determined to bring her up in a disciplined manner, and naturally she always got her own way, rather like today, because she is absolutely irresistible! I'm delighted, too, that Stephen has found her equally irresistible and I am thrilled to welcome him to the family.

I know other people want to say a few words, so Claire, Stephen, can I just say that you are two wonderful people and I hope you have a wonderful life together. Ladies and gentlemen, please join me in a toast to the bride and groom!

The groom's speech

**You have proposed, helped plan the day and
can't wait for your honeymoon** but, before you
can party the night away, it's time to say a few words.
Traditionally, your speech comes between the father
of the bride's and the best man's. It provides you, as
a couple, with the opportunity to say thank you to all
the people who have helped organize the wedding,
and to present them with gifts. It also gives you
a chance to reflect on the event that has brought
everyone together. You may well want to talk about
how you met your bride, relate some funny and/or
touching anecdotes describing how your romance
developed, and perhaps say something about the
nature of love and marriage in general.

You will say the most important words of the day, if not your life, when you say 'I do'. Now it's your chance to thank everybody and tell your bride how much you love her, and in front of everybody you know. Daunted? Don't be – everybody is there because they want to be. They've chosen to spend their free time watching you marry the woman you love and, for once, the focus is not on her dress but on you.

For many grooms, the speech can cause something of a dilemma. On one hand, a wedding is the occasion for expressing love for your new wife and gratitude to both sets of parents but, on the other hand, you don't want to come across as too sentimental in front of friends! Therefore, it would be helpful to plan your speech as a happy medium between the two.

Remember that if your bride is not going to give a speech, all your words should be from both of you. Bear this in mind throughout your speech – you don't want to just include your new wife in a single section of it as if you'd only just remembered to bung her in at the last minute! Oh – and beginning your speech 'My wife and I...' usually provokes an immediate audience reaction!

Where to start

So, what is expected of the groom?

- The first task is to thank your new father-in-law for his speech and for his beautiful daughter.
- Thank the guests for sharing your day and for their generous gifts.
- Thank both sets of parents for their help with the wedding celebrations.
- Give a small gift to the two mothers. (For some suggestions, see www.confetti.co.uk/speeches/p35**)**
- Compliment your new wife!
- Thank the best man for his help, and give your gifts to him and to the rest of the bridal party.
- Raise a glass and offer a toast to the bridesmaids.

Here are some useful phrases and ideas for a great groom's speech. All you need to do is pick the best ones for you and fill in the blanks!

1. Thank your new father-in-law

- I just want to thank my father-in-law for his *kind/ generous/special* words. I feel honoured that he has *taken/welcomed* me into his family.
- Thank you, Ken, for your *kind/generous/sweet/special* words. It is good to know how you feel about Sarah and me getting married.
- My wife and I would like to thank Ken for being the best father of the bride ever. Not only did he give her away instead of locking her in her room, but his *kind/sweet/ generous/witty* words have also made me feel welcome as the newest member of his family.
- My wife and I want to thank Ken for his *witty/kind/ generous/sincere* words. I now feel *embarrassed about everything I said about him in the past/justified in my opinion that he's a great/good/perfect father-in-law*. What can I say after that speech? Thanks, Ken.

2. Thank your guests

- This is the most important day of our lives, and *my wife and I/Sarah and I/we* are delighted to share it with *so many friends and family/our closest friends and families/two complete strangers in a register office*. We are also very grateful that so many of you have not only gone to the expense of sharing this day with us but have also bought us presents. Thank you.

- I can't believe that you all made it here. You really are the best *bunch/group/lot/mob/pack/herd* of friends and family that we could ever hope to have. So thank you. We're also extremely grateful for the presents. Sarah was saying only a couple of days ago that she really wanted another toaster... or two!

3. Thank your in-laws

- I am so *delighted/pleased/honoured/relieved/happy* to have Ken and Angela as my *new family/in-laws/other Mum and Dad*. I knew that I'd *like/love/get on with/ adore* them when I fell in love with Sarah because they have helped her to be the person she is – *perfect/rich/ wonderful/fond of beer and rugby!*

4. Compliment your wife!

- You are always beautiful but you have never looked as *stunning/good/wonderful/gorgeous* as you do today. You make the most *wonderful/stunning/gorgeous/ perfect* bride. I love you.
- I was expecting to feel *nervous/sick/terrified/concerned/ worried/frightened* when I woke up today but I didn't. Why? Because I knew that you would be walking down that aisle towards me and that the only thing I wanted was for *you to be my wife/us to be married*. I knew that you would look lovely – you always do – but today you are *radiant/gorgeous/beautiful/wonderful/fantastic/ stunning/a vision/perfect/the perfect bride*. You mean so much to me, and I want to thank you for agreeing to become my wife. I am so *proud/happy/honoured* to be your husband, and I love you very much.

- Sarah, you are a **beautiful/stunning/radiant/gorgeous/ lovely** bride, and I know that you are just as beautiful on the inside. When we first met, I realized that you **were the most beautiful woman in the world/were the only woman for me/had a ladder in your stockings**, but I never **thought/imagined/dared to hope** that you would marry me. I am so **happy/chuffed/delighted/ecstatic/ proud** that you agreed to be my wife and share the rest of your life with me. I've been so proud of the way you have juggled organizing this wedding with **your job/ everything else** and have still been patient and understanding. Now, I just want to say, in front of our friends and family, how much you mean to me. I love you.

5. Thank your bride

- I never thought I could be as happy as I am today without **England/Wales/Scotland/Ireland** winning the Six Nations. Roz, you've made me feel like I've **scored the winning try/kicked a critical drop goal** in the match of my life. You're my **Twickenham/Millennium Stadium/ Murrayfield/Landsdown Road**, and right now I feel like cheering because I'm just over the moon you've married me. I know there will be times when you send me **for an early bath/to sit in the sin bin**. But I also know that, just like supporting Bath, it's something that stays with you for life, through the ups and downs, and you just can't change that. Roz, I'm your biggest fan, and I love you.
  (You can amend the above to reflect your favourite sport – but only use it if it's not a sore spot with the bride!)

6. Thank the best man

- When I asked Sarah to marry me, I knew that I needed a best man and that there was only one man that title could be given to. Bob *is my brother and also a friend/ has been my best friend since school/1972/we met in the sandpit/he stole my BMX*, and I knew that he would be perfect for the job. I would like to thank him for all the work he's done today – *acting as toastmaster/not losing the rings/getting me to the church on time/ finding my trousers* – and for his efforts before the wedding when he listened to me as I raved about the latest *waistcoat/buttonhole/wedding dress* I had seen. Bob, you've been *great/a mate/the best man I could have chosen/cool/a pal/a true friend/gorgeous!*

- I get the fun parts of today, but Bob has all the stressful parts. As he's the *local postie/hippo-keeper/accountant/ general layabout*, I knew that he would be more than able to cope with today and keep everything, especially me, ticking along smoothly.

7. Thank and toast the bridesmaids

- The *giggling little posse/stunning group* of beautiful bridesmaids *over there/to my right/to my left/in front of you* have been amazing. Not only did they manage to walk down the aisle without falling over, but they've also been great with all the preparations. It may seem unfair to the rest of you, as you've all been *so great/helpful/ amazing/bored rigid*, but I'd particularly like to thank Vikki for all her hard work. I understand that Sarah's dress would not be looking quite so *beautiful/stunning/ together/white* as it does now were it not for a timely intervention! Ladies and gentleman, I'd like you all to *charge/raise* your glasses. I give you… the bridesmaids.

- *My wife and I/Sarah and I* would like to say a special thank you to the bridesmaids, who have been a tower of strength throughout the *preparations/day*. They've been *great/wonderful/beautiful*, and little Anna has been so *good/patient/sweet* and looks *gorgeous/adorable/very grown up* in her dress. Ladies and gentlemen, please *charge/raise* your glasses. I give you… the bridesmaids.

For more information about the groom's role and duties, go to www.confetti.co.uk/speeches/p41

SAMPLE SPEECHES: Sweet and loving

As Jane Austen, or was it Bridget Jones, said 'It is a truth universally acknowledged that a single man in possession of a good fortune must be in want of a good wife.'

Now much as I like to think I am Mr D'Arcy, and that only bouncing a few cheques to the florist for today establishes me as a man of good fortune, my real good fortune in life is undoubtedly meeting, and marrying my wife, Chloe.

She certainly, as somebody else said, has a price beyond rubies, and I'd like to thank my new father in law for his kind words and his making me the richest man in the world by letting me marry her.

You have all helped make today the happiest day of our lives by being here with us and being kind enough to bring gifts. I never knew that toasters came in so many varieties! Seriously, the greatest gift to us is your being here, and I hope that you enjoy the day half as much as we are.

My wife (I love saying that!) would not be the person she is without the love and support of her parents, and I want to thank them for helping her to be her and for welcoming me into their family. As my new mother-in-law said, she is not losing a daughter but gaining a washer-upper. While not quite so useful, I hope that she will accept this small gift as a sign of how much I appreciate her love and support, especially through the nerve-wracking preparations for the wedding.

All that hard work was worth it. Sarah looks even more beautiful than she does normally, and I hope that I will be everything she could ever hope for in a husband. If there is one thing I have learnt from her, it is patience, and today was worth all the waiting.

Sarah, I just want to say, in front of our families and dearest friends, that I love you and hope that every day will be as happy as today – just not as expensive.

Not only did Bob, my old roommate from Uni days and the best man I know, get me to the church on time but he also didn't lose the ring. I'm grateful for everything that he's done for me and look forward to returning the compliment – as soon as possible.

Lastly, I would like to thank the pack of bridesmaids, who have been such good friends throughout all the preparations. In particular, I would like to thank Vikki, the chief bridesmaid, who has been there every step of the way, from the wedding dress shop to the hairdressers, offering advice and support, even if it was only to mutter something about looking like a meringue! Please accept these flowers in thanks for everything you've done.

Ladies and gentlemen, please be upstanding. I give you... the bridesmaids.

SAMPLE SPEECHES: **Short and sweet**

Having listened to such words of wisdom from my new father-in-law, I can only hope that I am worthy of them. Thank you, Ken.

I'm really pleased that you could all make it here today, but I'm especially grateful to the Johnsons, who've travelled all the way from Edinburgh to be with us. I knew that it was worth including the words 'free bar' on the invitations!

You've all been very generous, not only by being here today to share this happy occasion, but also by giving us so many wonderful gifts.

My parents brought me up to believe that good things come to those who wait, and I want to thank them for being right and for being there whenever I needed them, especially this morning when Dad helped me do up my tie as I was shaking so much. Thanks, both of you.

I now have a new set of parents, the in-laws. Contrary to all the horror stories, mine are amazing, but I always knew that they would be as no one could raise so perfect a woman as my wife if they weren't wonderful themselves. I want to thank them for helping us to have the best wedding we could ever have dreamed of. Thank you, Ken and Angela, for your kindness and for raising such a beautiful daughter.

Sarah, no one could have made me as happy as you have these last few years, and I look forward to growing old and grey with you.

And going grey is something that almost happened prematurely when we were on the way to the church and Bob realized that he'd left the ring behind. Fortunately, everything else went according to plan, and it was great to have my best man at my side.

As for the bridesmaids, what can I say except they look lovely and have been great through all the preparations? I'd like them to accept these small offerings with our love. They deserve a drink so, ladies and gentlemen, please be upstanding. I give you... the bridesmaids.

SAMPLE SPEECHES: Second marriages

This is a second marriage for both of us, and I am grateful for the words my new father-in-law has just spoken. Sarah and I feel privileged to have found each other and to be given a second chance of love.

My parents have been particularly supportive over the last few weeks when wedding nerves set in, but this was to be expected as they've always been there for me, no matter what. I know that Sarah feels the same about her parents, who have welcomed me into their family and have been so generous, helping us with this wedding.

When I first met Sarah I thought that she was a beautiful woman but I never thought I'd see her again. Fortunately, thanks to some matchmaking by Bob, my best man and the father of Billy, our excellent pageboy who only tried to eat the cushion once, we did see each other again. I'd like to thank him for helping us get where we are today. Sarah and I will always be grateful for his interference!

Sarah believes strongly that looks are less important than personality, which is just as well, otherwise she wouldn't have agreed to marry me! Sarah has taught me the importance of patience and compromise as our families have united to make a whole, and I am grateful to her that she has helped me make this transition quite so easily. Standing here today, in front of you all, I have to say that it has definitely been worth it.

Obviously our wedding would be nothing without the love and blessing of our children: Claire, David and Simon. Claire has told me confidentially, so you'll have to keep this to yourselves, that she's always wanted a brother. So now that she's got two, I hope that she'll be twice as happy. David and Simon, I'd like to say how delighted I am to be your step-father. And Claire, Sarah has asked me to say that you are the daughter she thought she would never have.

Sarah's sister, Vikki, has been a tower of strength through all the pre-wedding stress. So for that and for your fantastic flower arrangements, thank you, Vikki. And for those of you who are wondering how we spent the money that we saved on the flowers, we spent it on extra booze! So, take advantage and raise your glasses to... Bob and Vikki.

How to include children of a previous marriage

- I've always been terribly grateful to Sara's children, Fiona and Jack. Sarah's experience raising them has surely made her more prepared to take me on, although I do promise to clean my room and do my homework from now on.
- I'm delighted that my sons John and Peter and Sasha's daughter Melanie are here to share today – and the rest of our lives – with us. They're wonderful people.
- I count myself doubly lucky that the young lady over there, Tina, Geraldine's daughter, can be with us today. It is a delight and a privilege to know her, and thank you, Tina, for all the help you've given us preparing for this wedding.

SAMPLE SPEECHES: Personal and humorous

That was a hard act to follow. I hope I'll be able to look after Felicity as well as you have, Dick.

Thank you all for coming here today, especially everyone who has travelled from the other side of the Atlantic to share this day with us. May I just let you all know we think Guildford is quite a large town around here, so please stop referring to it as 'cute' and 'quaint' and saying how nice it would look in the back yard.

Thank you also for your generous gifts. We're actually a bit upset, as we threw out our old toaster yesterday in anticipation of receiving several more. We've opened most of the gifts and no one seems to have given us one.

Of course, none of us would be here today without Felicity's parents – Shirley and Dick – and my parents – Flora and Johnny. When I met Felicity, I thought she was sincere, kind and caring, and when I met her parents, I knew exactly where she got it from. It's clearly genetic, and I hope our children will inherit it.

Flora and Johnny have been so supportive to me – always. I've worried sometimes that I'm not good enough for Felicity, but my mum has always assured me I am. And even though I know she's biased, I was egotistical enough to believe her, and here I am today. So, Shirley and Flora, we'd like to give you these little tokens of our love and thanks.

My love and thanks today really have to go to Felicity —
for being here, for being so beautiful and for being my wife.
As an investment banker, Felicity deals with mergers and
acquisitions. On this occasion, I'm thrilled she's mixed business
with pleasure and merged with my family and acquired me!

You've all met Aloysius, my best man. When I asked him to
be my best man, I checked with him that he could organize
a stag night, make a speech, even get me to the church on
time. But I forgot to ask the most important thing: could
he tie the knot? I'm not talking about marriage here — I'm
talking about the horrendous mess he's made of my bow tie!

Thank you also to the beautiful bridesmaids. I know they and
Oddbins have been a great support to Felicity during the last
few months. Felicity, Laura, Sarah, Johanna and Chardonnay
met up so often I was confused as to why there are only
three bridesmaids here today.

Ladies and gentlemen, Chardonnay could not be with us
today, but Champagne has kindly stepped into the breach,
so if you would all raise your glasses. I give you… the
bridesmaids!

SAMPLE SPEECHES: **Other nickable lines!**
**If you're still stuck for ideas, here are some lines
from other grooms' speeches that you may want
to 'borrow'.**

Thanking guests

- I am overwhelmed by how many of you came today, and I want you to know how much my wife and I appreciate you all being here to share this day with us. As for the gifts, you really are a generous bunch.
- The trouble with weddings, or so I've been told, is that you never have the time to say how much you appreciate seeing everyone. So, I'm going to speak for both of us when I say how much I appreciate you all taking the time to be here today. And thank you so much for your generous presents. We will be circulating later and hope to have the chance to talk to all of you.

Thanking parents

- When I saw Ken looking so proud as he walked down the aisle with Sarah, I realized how much the day means to both Angela and him. Sarah is their daughter, and this is the moment they've been looking forward to ever since she was a little girl. I hope that they will be as happy to have me as their son-in-law as I am to have them as my parents-in-law. I just want to reassure them that I love Sarah and will do everything in my power to make her as happy for the rest of her life as I know she is today.

- Mum's a bit *miffed/upset/annoyed* as she wanted to give me away but had to wear a hat instead! My mum and dad have been great, and I'd like to thank them for all the support they have given me over the years and for their kindness towards Sarah. I know that she really loves having you as her new in-laws.
- When I proposed to Sarah, I did so in the knowledge that, not only do I love her, but also that marriage can be the most wonderful thing in the world. I know that because my parents have been married for 30 years and are still in love. I hope that Sarah and I can be as happy as the two of you. You really are the best parents anyone could ever have, and I love you.

To the bride

- Sarah, you know that I love you, and I hope that by marrying you today, in front of everyone we care about, you will see just how much you mean to me. You are my sunshine, and without you the world would be a gloomy place. I am so proud to be your husband, and I want us to grow old and grey together. We have so many plans for our future but, whatever happens, I know that we will be together for ever.
- Sarah, or as I should now say, Mrs Smith, I couldn't believe my luck when you first agreed to go out with me. Two years later, when you said that you would marry me, I knew I was a really lucky bloke. Now that you are my wife, I've got everything I ever wanted, and I'm looking forward to spending the rest of my life with you.

The best man's speech

Of all the traditional speeches at the wedding reception, the best man's is usually the most eagerly anticipated. Guests look for humour in all the speeches, and are generally happy to reward even the feeblest attempt at a joke with gales of booming laughter. But the expectation is that, whether or not any of the other speakers can stretch to a gag, the best man should do his level best to put on a bit of a show and raise a few chuckles.

The best man usually speaks last, by which time guests tend to have relaxed considerably (a fact not unconnected with the wine that is disappearing at a rapid rate from the tables). Their sense of humour threshold will have lowered considerably, so anything that seems even vaguely like a punch line should bring the house down.

Another advantage you'll have at this point is familiarity. Usually – unless you have a separate Master of Ceremonies – you, the best man, will have been acting as the host or anchorman of the whole occasion, so by the time you get up to say your piece, guests will be used to your ways.

Your role is, in fact, a multiple one. As the groom's best friend, it is your job to humiliate the main man in as amusing a fashion as possible. As host, you will read out telegrams and pass on any practical announcements – anything people need to know, for instance, plans for the evening's activities. And, as traditional head of the wedding assistants, you will also speak on behalf of the bridesmaids.

The most important thing to remember, though, is to relax – the groom wouldn't have asked you to be his best man if he hadn't thought that you could cope. So, just do what comes naturally – be witty and say what you think – but within reason.

Where to start

So, what is expected of the best man?

- Thank the groom for his toast on behalf of the bridesmaids and for any gifts that were presented.
- Comment on the bride and groom – you could mention how great they look today or why they're so compatible.
- Compliment the groom. Brides always get a lot of the attention at weddings, and this point in your speech is a good place to redress the balance a little.
- Try to amuse the guests with anecdotes about the groom's misdemeanours in the past or with jokes at the groom's expense.
- Read any messages that have been received from absent friends and family.
- Raise a glass and offer a toast to the bride and groom.
- If the bride is making a speech, you will need to perform one further function, which is to introduce the bride.

Here are some useful phrases and ideas for a best man's speech. All you need to do is pick the best ones for you and fill in the blanks!

1. The thanks

You represent the other members of the bridal party (i.e. the bridesmaids and ushers), so the first thing you have to say is easy – thank the groom for his words about the bridesmaids.

- Ladies and gentlemen, I would like to thank the groom for his *kind/generous/short/patronizing/lying* words about the *lovely/giggling/drunken/fabulous* bridesmaids.

2. Who are you?

Let everyone know how you and the groom first met each other and how you feel about being his best man.

- When I first met John on our first day at *school/Uni/ prison/work*, I thought that he was *a good bloke/a con man/an idiot/an alcoholic/a lucky man to meet me*, but I never realized that I would end up, all these years later, being his best man. I have to say that I was *honoured/staggered/horrified/shocked/drunk* when he asked me, but I'm *delighted/honoured/pleased/drunk again/terrified* to be here today in front of all of you.

3. About the groom

- John has always been *a good bloke/an idiot/a generous man*, even when *[say when you met, e.g., first day of school]* and he *[recount a funny incident or use one of his pet phrases; don't cause offence but be funny]*. I can't believe that he's *finally/actually* married.

- When John asked me to be his best man I thought that *he had no other friends/his Mum had made him ask me*, and I was *honoured/terrified*. Now that I'm here, I'm even more so.

- The man who wouldn't *commit/buy pizza for more than one/share his remote control/even consider a joint bank account* is now married!

- I never thought that I'd live to see this day. I've known John since *[say how you met and when]* and I'm *delighted/stunned/pleased/shocked/really happy for him* and even more *shocked at/horrified at/staggered by/terrified by/committed to* being his best man – as he is the best man I've ever known.

4. Tell an amusing/sweet anecdote about the groom

You're his best man for a reason, so delve into your mutual past and tell an amusing anecdote. Hopefully, the only difficulty doing this is trying to decide which tale to tell. If it's not that easy, the following might trigger a few memories – just remember to keep it short and clean!

- Thinking up an original excuse for being late/not handing in his homework/project.
- First time you had a boy's night out and he decided that he wanted to be a morris dancer.
- Any dreams of unsuitable jobs, e.g. pilot, stripper [unless he was!], train/racing driver [and recently had a minor scrape in his car], pop star [and can't sing], etc.
- Cooking anecdotes always work. The late Dame Barbara Cartland once said that 90% of marriages end because of bad cooking, and even if he didn't blow up a microwave by putting a whole egg in it, he must have had some kind of cooking disaster – we all have. As the 19th-century poet George Meredith said, 'Kissing don't last: cookery do!'

5. Don't forget the bride

Always make a point of saying something nice about the bride. This is the woman who will let your friend/brother still go out to play with the lads, so start off on the right foot. You know you want to!

- *Sarah/Mrs Finn* is the luckiest *woman/girl* for marrying John today but, looking at her, I can understand why he chose her. She's a *beautiful/stunning/gorgeous/lovely/radiant* bride.
- Sarah, what can I say? You look *beautiful/lovely/stunning/radiant* and you *deserve each other/make a beautiful couple/are perfect for each other*.
- When John first introduced me to Sarah, my first reaction was that she was *too good/perfect/ideal* for him. I'm delighted to see them here together today and wish them every happiness for the future.

6. Telegram time

A simple rule: explain who all the telegrams are from. Bill and Joy Patterson may mean nothing to many people but saying Uncle Bill and Aunt Joy from Scotland will make it easier for everyone.

7. Almost there – the final toast

It's nearly time to sit down, but not just yet. This is the easy bit and your audience will be delighted to participate. Decide with the bride and groom beforehand if people should stand up or not. If they should, ask them to 'be upstanding'.

- Ladies and gentlemen, please be upstanding and *raise/ charge* your glasses. I give you... the bride and groom.
- Ladies and gentlemen, please join me in a toast. I give you... the bride and groom.

Do's and don'ts

- Never swear or use offensive words, even if they do crop up in everyday speech.
- Always think of an old granny sitting in the corner when you write your speech and try not to give her a heart attack or make her blush!
- Don't try too hard to be funny.
- Avoid saying anything you wouldn't want anyone to know if it were about you and you can't go wrong.
- Make a note of anyone you want to thank or mention. You might find it easiest to write down your speech to either glancing at or as reassurance, or use little revision cards with bullet point reminders.
- Decide if you want to read some cards or telegrams during your speech. If you do, be sure to arrange for a family member to collect them together for you.
- Practise, practise, practise!
- Never make fun of the wedding, even if you dislike the venue, colour scheme, even the bride's dress.
- Avoid potentially difficult and embarrassing subjects like having children (in case it turns out that they can't), drug problems (in case either the bride or the families don't know about it), excessive partying or womanizing while seeing the bride (ditto), money problems (ditto) or previous girlfriends (need we say more?).

For more information about the best man's role and duties, go to www.confetti.co.uk/speeches/p61

SAMPLE SPEECHES: Cool and collected

I'd like to thank John for his kind words about the bridesmaids and wondered if anyone can tell me if it's true that the chief bridesmaid has to kiss the best man as part of tradition – I'd hate to break with tradition!

I've known some of you for years, and I know that John appreciates all of you being here – both old friends and new. We've been friends since our first day of secondary school and we're friends for a reason – because he's a good man, and Sarah's very lucky to have caught him!

When John told me that he was marrying Sarah, I thought, 'That's great, party time.' When he asked me to be his best man, I thought, 'Oh no, emigrate!' But I didn't. Why? Because I couldn't let him down. This is the man who taught me how to play poker when we were 11 and then fleeced me.

I tried to convince him to bet Sarah in a game last night but he refused. He even cried when he said, after several whiskies, I might add, how much he loved her. Sarah, I'll spare your blushes, but I'm delighted to know that the two of you are so… compatible [suggest something jokingly without being crude].

I remember when John was being taught biology and got a little confused about the birds and the bees. He asked why any bird would want to date a bee and, on a similar note,

I bet that some of you are wondering what on earth someone as beautiful as Sarah sees in my old mate. John is here as the groom but, in my opinion, he's the best man, not me. He's a kind, generous friend who cannot do enough for those he cares about – that includes visiting his grandfather in the nursing home every fortnight, helping his mum with her lawn and bailing me out of one or two scrapes. John has always been there for me, and I'd like to thank him for everything he's ever done for all of us.

John, you're a good man and you deserve the best. With Sarah, you've got it, and I wish you every happiness.

Before we get to the toast and, believe me, I need a drink – it's terrifying up here – I'd like to read out a few telegrams from those people who missed this bash, which is the best wedding I've ever been to, from these fantastic guests to the wonderful drinks. And some of you look lov-e-ly after such good champagne!

There are some great telegrams from people who really care about you, and I know that we all wish you two the greatest happiness. Ladies and gentlemen, please be upstanding and raise your glasses. I give you… the bride and groom.

SAMPLE SPEECHES: Not the nine o'clock news
Alternatively, you could run the speech like a news report to tie in any anecdotes from the groom's life. For example:

- *Headlines*
  We don't like to mention the headlines because John is very sensitive about having his bald spot pointed out.
- *Education news*
  This is the perfect opportunity to drop in a story about school or college.
- *Now for the sports news*
  John is a huge Arsenal fan. Despite being slightly overweight for a professional, not having played for ten years and more familiar with table football than Wembley Stadium, John still dreams of being called up to play with Tony Adams.
- *Travel hotspots*
  A quick tale from a lads' holiday/tease him about his driving technique/an anecdote about the groom resembling British Rail and always running late.
- *News just in*
  Read the telegrams and cards from absent friends.

SAMPLE SPEECHES: **Other nickable lines**
Still looking for inspiration? Here is a collection
of lines from various best man speeches that are
perfectly pinchable.

1. The opener

- First, an apology. Due to an electrical problem, the speakers' voices may sound a little jittery. This has absolutely nothing to do with nerves.

- Asking someone to be your best man is one of the greatest honours you can bestow, but it's also a terrible thing to do to a friend. Thanks guys.

- On behalf of the bridesmaids (who, incidentally, are still waiting for an official invite) and the ushers, I would like to thank John for his kind words and wish him and Sarah many years of happiness together. Do I get paid yet?

- Let me take a second to introduce myself... I am John's *old friend/brother/college mate*, who only behaves well when holding a pint. As I will be found in the not-too-distant future somewhere near the bar, please do not hesitate to come and introduce yourself.

2. The gentle joke

- Thank you to the Rabbi for a wonderful service. You may be amused to know that at the rehearsal he told our esteemed groom that, when he stamps on the glass, it would be the last time he puts his foot down with Sarah. As far as I am aware, it was also the first time!
- I can now reveal that John slept like a baby last night… He woke up crying every half hour, wanting his mummy.

3. The groom – how to start embarrassing stories

- It is with great pride that I stand before you charged with embarrassing John. John… I have waited 32 years for this moment and I am going to savour every second of it! [Turn to the bride and groom and say:] This is my final offer – £20 to skip the next bit!
- Ladies and gentlemen, let me begin by putting John out of his misery. John, I want you to know that I thought about taking a tour of your pre-wedding closet and bringing out a few skeletons. But it's not going to happen. That's not what this is all about. I won't mention the special name his primary school girlfriend had for him. I won't mention what he did when he was 11 that scandalized the neighbours. And whatever he's done with sheep, rubber chickens and a plastic doll called Annie in the past… well, they're his business.'

- Ladies and gentlemen, I want to thank the bride and groom for many things. The bride is truly beautiful and this wedding is magnificent, but it's also very important to me to admit in public that everything vital in life that I've learned in the last ten years, I've learned from you. So touched am I by the impression you've made on me that I think those lessons are too good to keep to ourselves, so today I thought I'd share them with everyone here. Thanks to John, I know that life is so much more enjoyable if **you're prepared to admit when you're wrong/you're a charmer/you understand women/you work hard/you study hard.**

4. Surprise, surprise

- Oh, and I also have a letter for John from Italy:

Mio amore Gianni,
I am so pleased to have found an address for you. From the moment we first met during a school exchange holiday in Italy I have always held you close to my heart. Since you visited last month – did anyone believe you were working in Birmingham? – I have moved to Rome. The baby is well, but I am struggling to look after him on my own. Could you spare some lire or, even better, come and see us again?

Forever yours
Francesca

The bride's speech

The bride doesn't traditionally take part in the formal speeches, but if you want to be more than just a pretty dress and add a few words of your own, then the best time to do so is after your groom or the best man. More and more brides now choose to give a personal speech, and it can be a great way of mopping up any forgotten thank yous. Even if you've decided not to make a speech, it's a good idea to have something in mind, as you might find that your guests start calling for you to say a few words!

As the bride, you have the most interesting role of all when it comes to the speeches. Whereas the roles of the other main speakers, such as the father of the bride and the best man, have huge traditions attached to them – father dotes on daughter, best man humiliates groom, and so on – you and your speech labour under no such burden of expectation. This is because – although it's by no means uncommon any more – the bride's speech is still a very new development in terms of the history of wedding procedure. And that means you still have the choice to say pretty much what you like and when you like. It's your call.

If your father is not present, then you may want to speak first of all, in the traditional father-of-the-bride slot. Some couples opt to stand up and speak together (in many ways, a very logical choice); others prefer to speak separately, and each addresses different themes (the other's family, for instance). Or you may prefer to speak after your husband, or even after the best man, as the very last speaker.

Where to start

So, what is expected of the bride?

- Thank everyone who's attending, especially long-lost friends and people who've travelled a long way.
- Thank those people who've supported you through the stress of preparing for the wedding.
- A special word about your mum, not just to thank her for her role in the wedding preparations, but to describe your relationship with her over the years.
- If you like, you could echo the pattern of your new husband's speech: how you met; your first impressions; things you liked and didn't like about him; how the relationship developed; your thoughts on love and marriage; a more personal message from you to him.
- Thank your guests for all their gifts (if the groom hasn't done so already).
- If you are thanking other people, it might make more sense for you, rather than the groom, to thank the bridesmaids.
- A popular American innovation is for the bride to finish with a toast to the guests.

For more information about the bride's role, go to www.confetti.co.uk/speeches/p71

SAMPLE SPEECH: **Short and fun**

I feel like a winner on Oscar night – there are so many people to thank. I just want to reiterate all the thanks that have gone on before. Mum and dad, you've been great, as have my new in-laws. Thanks to Bob and Vikki, who've helped us to hold this wedding together, and to all of you for just being here, especially that noisy group in the corner who grew up with me and remember how often I said I'd never get married. But, most of all, I'd like to thank John for asking me to marry him and then going through with it!

You've all been so kind saying how nice I look, but I just wanted to say how gorgeous John looks today in his suit. You're great, darling.

I know you all want to get back to the champagne, so I'll leave you to it, but thanks so much for being here and making our day so special.

I'd like you all to raise your glasses and drink a toast... to friends and family.

SAMPLE SPEECH: Short and sweet

We're gathered here today to watch John agree to a lifetime of housework and pampering me! I thought about reading out a poem, but I couldn't find one that came close to conveying how happy I am today, with my dearest friends and family around me to see me marry the man I love. Thank you. Please join me in a toast… to love and friendship.

SAMPLE SPEECH: When you have lost a parent

This is the best day of my life, but it is also a very difficult one. Dad died over a year ago, but I miss him more today than I ever have. This would have been his special day, too, and he would have been so proud to walk me down the aisle on his arm.

But I am also happy, as dad would have wanted me to be. I am marrying the man I love, and I hope that we will always have the love we have today and be as happy as our parents.

John, thank you for supporting me through rough times as well as happy ones, and thank you for today. I love you.

Alternatively, you could say the following:
I just wanted to say how much I wish Dad were here to enjoy this day as much as we have and to embarrass me with memories probably best left forgotten. I know that, wherever he is, he is looking down on us and smiling. I also want to thank Uncle Paul for walking me down the aisle.

You've all made me so happy just by being here, and I can't believe Don and Mary, my old flatmates from Uni, have come all the way over from America – you're brilliant.

Mostly, I'd like to thank John just for asking – although it took him long enough!

I'd also like to make a toast. Please lift your glasses and drink to absent friends.

SAMPLE SPEECH: Poetry please
Instead of making a speech, you may find it easier
to read out a poem, like the following:

To My Dear Loving Husband
by Anne Bradstreet (1612–1672)
If ever two were one, then surely we.
If ever man were loved by wife, then thee;
If ever wife was happy in a man,
Compare with me, ye woman, if you can.
I prize thy love more than whole mines of gold
Or all the riches that the East doth hold.
My love is such that rivers cannot quench,
Nor ought but love from thee, give recompense.
Thy love is such I can no way repay,
The heavens reward thee manifold, I pray.
The while we live, in love let's so persevere,
That when we live no more, we may live ever.

If you'd like some more suggestions for appropriate poetry
and prose, the confetti.co.uk book *Wedding Readings* has a
wide selection from which to choose.

Stepping into the breach

Standing in for the father of the bride or the best man can be a tricky job. If you're lucky, you will have been warned in plenty of time, but if you're a last-minute substitute, don't worry, there is still time to prepare an excellent speech.

Perhaps the family would prefer a close friend to speak rather than a parent, or perhaps you are a recent step-parent or have been asked to speak in the unfortunate event of the father's death or absence. Maybe the best man has pulled out at the last minute. Whatever the reason, if you are the person to stand and make that speech, then this is the chapter for you.

The key speeches at any wedding might not always be given by the obvious first choice. The father of the bride, for instance, may be estranged from his daughter's family or he may have died before her wedding. Likewise, an illness or accident may deprive the reception of its best man or chief bridesmaid.

In these and many other circumstances, the families of the bride and groom may need to find a replacement speaker. As the wedding day approaches, they will start to look around among friends and family for suitable stand-ins. And this is when you may find yourself asked to give a speech on behalf of someone else. Here's what you need to know and do to survive the experience.

Where to start

So, what is expected of a stand-in speaker?

- Introduce yourself and explain briefly your relationship to the bride (and groom).
- If one of the bride or groom's parents has passed away, you should honour them in your speech. See page 29 for ideas on how to do this.
- Thank the guests for joining the celebrations.
- Thank all those who have paid for any part of the wedding and helped to organize the day.
- Compliment the bride.
- Welcome the groom.
- Propose a toast to the bride and groom.

If you have been asked to give the first speech, you will probably have known the bride for a number of years, but still take the time to speak to her family beforehand, especially her mother, who, traditionally, plays a silent role on the day. The following are a few options to cut and paste into your own speech.

1. The introduction

- I am delighted to be here and feel very privileged to have been Nicola's step-father for the last 15 years.
- I feel very honoured to stand here and speak on behalf of my father, who would have loved to see my sister Nicola marry John.
- As Nicola's godfather, I've been asked by her parents to welcome you all to her wedding and say a few words about their beautiful daughter.

2. The thanks

- Ladies and gentlemen, I'd like to thank you all for being here today to witness the marriage of Nicola and John.
- Ladies and gentlemen, I'm delighted to see so many of you here today to share this special day with Nicola and John.
- Ladies and gentlemen, I know how delighted Nicola and John are to see so many of their friends and relatives on *their special day/the most important day of their lives*.

3. Thanking contributors

- Today would not have been possible without the generous help of both sets of parents, Ken and Angela, and Fred and Jane, and I know that the couple are very grateful to them.
- Nicola and John have done a wonderful job with the wedding arrangements, but they would like to make a special mention of Vikki, who very generously donated the magnificent flowers.

4. Compliment the bride

Here, we have given you a few options to cut and paste into your own speech:

- I know that Ken and Angela are very proud of their daughter Nicola. She has worked extremely hard to get where she is today *[name her career or mention what she studied at university]* and she is a **beautiful/ radiant/gorgeous** bride. However, I will always remember her as *a scruffy/an inquisitive/a mischievous baby/ child/adolescent*.
- Nicola makes a **glamorous/radiant/gorgeous/lovely** bride but, to me, she will always be a **scruffy/mischievous/ solemn/beautiful baby/child/teenager.** Her family and friends are so proud of her, not only because she has been so successful in *[name her career/studying/hobbies or achievements],* but because she is *as beautiful on the inside as she is on the outside/a generous, warm-hearted and loving woman*.
- Seeing Nicola here today, looking so **beautiful/radiant/ happy**, I would never recognize the **baby/child/teenager** who loved nothing better than to *[tell a sweet anecdote, e.g. play with caterpillars/climb trees/play weddings with her dolls, etc.]*. I am **honoured/proud** to be here today speaking on behalf of her family, and I know that Ken and Angela are so proud that she has grown into such a **wonderful/sweet-natured/kind** woman.

5. Welcome the groom

- I am not only delighted for Nicola on her wedding day, but also for John. He is a good man and I know that Ken and Angela are delighted to welcome him into their family. Nicola and John make a beautiful couple and they have a lot in common. I am sure that they will be as happy in 20 years' time as they are today.

- John, you are the perfect man for Nicola. You are kind, warm-hearted and generous, and she deserves nothing less. On behalf of Ken and Angela, I am delighted to welcome you into the family.

- I've always thought that it would be difficult for Nicola to find a man who was worthy of her, but I was wrong. John is perfect for her, and I know that I speak on Ken and Angela's behalf when I say how delighted we all are that you have married Nicola.

6. Toast the bride and groom

Wait for all of the glasses to be filled before asking guests to stand for the first toast. Remember to wait for silence before starting the toast as you don't want to be drowned out by scraping chairs.

- Ladies and gentlemen, please be upstanding and raise your glasses. I give you... the bride and groom.
- Ladies and gentlemen, please be upstanding and charge your glasses. I give you... the bride and groom.
- Ladies and gentlemen, please be upstanding and join me in a toast to... the bride and groom.

If you're standing in for someone at the reception, chances are it's the father of the bride or the best man. So, you may want to base your words on the type of speech usually given by them, while adding some words about your relationship to the couple.

SAMPLE SPEECH: **Standing in for the deceased father of the bride**

Thank you, everyone, for being here today with Fiona and Nicholas. I know they're thrilled to see so many of you, and I know I'm honoured to be here, too. There is, of course, one person who is missing, and that's my father, who would have been so proud of Fiona today. I know most of us can probably picture him sitting here with us, smoking a huge cigar and thinking up embarrassing stories to tell about his daughter. He'd probably also be asking her if she really needed all those flowers and whether she couldn't just wear the dress he bought her for her 18th birthday party!

On the subject of parties, I really want to thank Nicholas and my stepfather, Andrew, for the wonderful reception they have provided for us all. You can tell by the look on Fiona's face that it's exactly what she's been boring us all to death about – I mean, dreaming about – since she was a little girl.

One of the things I'm meant to be doing now is to tell some stories about Fiona when she was small that will entertain you all but not humiliate her too badly. Well, I just don't think it's possible for a younger brother to relate any such tales. I know only really bad, really embarrassing stories, and as I'm hoping to continue to be on speaking terms with Fiona and Nicholas, I've decided against telling any of them today – well, at least within her earshot.

What I will say, though, is that Fiona is the best sister you could possibly wish for. She's clever, funny, beautiful, talented, and has very good-looking friends. She's also very lucky to have found Nicholas. I know he's a great bloke because he used to put up with me wanting to tag along to the pub all the time, and he talked to me about football, even though he's not a Liverpool fan. Today is meant to be an opportunity to welcome Nicholas into the family but, of course, he's been part of our family for years now.

I won't keep you any longer because I know we're all keen to hear what the new husband has to say about the day, so, ladies and gentlemen, I give you the bride and groom!

SAMPLE SPEECH: Standing in for the best man

On behalf of the bridesmaids, I'd like to thank you, Ronald, for those kind words. As you can see, there's been a change to the cast as advertised. After the success of Ron's stag night, his best man, John Greene, whom many of us may know by reputation, if not personally, has had to leave the country, and he's asked me to step in and keep Ron company at the altar while he lies low in Brazil. Honestly, though, I know John was really looking forward to Ron's wedding – something to do with getting the competition married off, I think – and he's devastated that's he's unable to be here today, especially with all these lovely bridesmaids around. I've actually received a telegram from him. It says, 'Phil, stop. No, seriously, stop!' I've also got some messages for the bride and groom from other absent friends and relatives.

When I was asking around about the true meaning and importance of weddings, one woman told me something rather interesting. She said, 'Women like the simple things in life, like men.' Suddenly, the secret of Ron's attractiveness to Julia became clear. His idea of complexity is ordering a round in a pub with more than two different kinds of beer on tap.

I wish Ron and Julia much luck, although I think she'll be needing it more, and Ron's probably used up all his luck allowance just finding such a wonderful person to agree to be his wife. Ladies and gentlemen, please be upstanding for the bride and groom.

The chief bridesmaid's speech

Although the official speeches are made by the men in the wedding party, some bridesmaids like to say a few words, too. If you decide to break with tradition, then remember to keep it simple and have fun!

Some chief bridesmaids approach their speech in a similar way to the best man. In other words, as an opportunity not only to praise the groom on his choice of bride and to toast their future together, but also to tell a few tales about the bride and hint at the uproar of the hen night. It's important to remember, though, that a bridesmaid's speech is still quite a new idea, so keep it short and sweet.

As chief bridesmaid or maid/matron of honour, you may wish, or be called upon, to make a speech at the reception. However, if the bride is having a dinner for her hen night, or you are throwing her a bridal shower in the American tradition, you will probably be expected to make a speech then. If the couple have a dinner after their wedding rehearsal, it is also traditional for you to make a toast then.

If you are speaking on behalf of someone who is absent or has elected not to speak, you should follow the traditional structure of their speech, as this ensures all the right people get thanked in the right order! But if you are speaking as the chief bridesmaid, you have fewer compulsory elements to include, and the greater part of your speech can be about the bride, your relationship with her and her relationship with the groom.

Where to start

Obviously the formality of your speech depends on the formality of the occasion, but if you are the bride's sister, or your relationship with her as a very old friend is well known, then you can get away with poking a bit more fun at her!

- Compliment the bride, and thank her for choosing you as her chief bridesmaid.
- Comment on the preparations for the wedding – this is the time you have spent together, both in the run-up to the day and in the time directly before the ceremony.
- Share a memory of the bride that highlights an amusing or endearing part of her personality.
- Compliment the ushers on behalf of the bridesmaids.
- Toast the bride and groom.

SAMPLE SPEECH: Mr and Mrs

Well, she's done it. Nicola has finally found a man who deserves her and, as one of her oldest friends, I couldn't be happier for her.

I just wanted to say a few unbiased words about what a great friend she is. No matter how far away we are physically from each other, she is always there for me and always says the right thing. I hope I can do the same for her today on her most important day. We go way back to the time when her ideal man was Action Man, all muscles and no brain. Fortunately, she's grown up since then and has chosen a man who matches her in every capacity, which is a rare thing for any couple to find.

Nicola is one of the nicest people I know, and I'm delighted to add John to my list of new friends. I hope that you'll be very happy together.

A toast – I know it's been done before, but – please raise your glasses to… the bride and groom.

SAMPLE SPEECH: Short and snappy

Okay, John, I thought I'd make a few things clear from the start! Nicola needs to use the phone for long gossip sessions with her friends about how wonderful you are and you're expected to pick up the tab. She has the right to get annoyed when you want to watch football instead of going with her to the supermarket where she will wander aimlessly up and down every aisle, even though you only came in for pizza to eat in front of the football. She *will* get grumpy once a month and you have to realize that this has nothing to do with hormones but is entirely down to you. Okay, so it isn't, but she's a woman and has the right to behave like this.

Why? Because you married her, and I'm delighted that you have. I think that the pair of you make a lovely couple and you both look stunning. It's good to see both of you make an effort for a change.

I remember the day when Nick wouldn't wear anything apart from jeans, and I have a horrible feeling that she's probably got a pair on under her dress so she can slide down the banisters later. Some things never change, even though she is a responsible bank clerk now!

So, as her ***best friend/sister***, I'd like you to raise your glasses… to John and Nicola. May they always be as happy as they are today.

SAMPLE SPEECH: **Just a quickie**

I'm sure you'll be delighted that, as Nicola's chief bridesmaid, I have only one thing to say: John and Nicola, you've thanked me for being your bridesmaid but I want to thank you for letting us all be here to share in your happiness. You really are the best friends anyone could ever hope for, and you're perfect for each other. I know that you'll be really happy.

There is only one toast I could give, so please join me in raising your glasses to... the bride and groom.

SAMPLE SPEECH: **Heartfelt and funny**

You may think that you've heard all that needs to be said, but I haven't even started yet. Don't despair, though. I am not the stereotypical woman you men think can talk forever on any subject, although weddings have become something of a speciality of mine over the last 12 months!

I would just like to take this opportunity to say a heartfelt thank you to Abi for asking me to be her chief bridesmaid. I have never felt prouder in my life than today, as I watched my little brat of a sister make a miraculous transition into this beautiful, radiant woman. And there were times when we all thought that this would never happen – we couldn't believe that anyone would ever take her on, what with her history! Of course, I mean her history of accidents. Abi is the only person I know who, on the most important day of her life, manages to spill hot tea on her foot, trip up the stairs, slip in the bathroom, fall over her slippers and then put the heel of her shoe through the hem of her petticoat. And all that in the course of one morning. Thankfully these were all minor mishaps and she has got through the day in one piece. Sadly, the same cannot be said for the cat…. My only word of advice to you, Matt, is to make sure that you are both well insured – you may need it.

We have all heard the lovely compliments paid to the bridesmaids, and I thank Robert (the best man) on their behalf. I would like to return the compliment and say how handsome the groomsmen look in their morning suits. However, I am amazed that Tony (the chief usher) is wearing a matching outfit, as I did have to explain to him that it was a morning suit, not a mourning suit, and we were going to celebrate Matt and Abi's wedding, not bury them. Still, it is wonderful to see that he has gone to so much trouble to look good, with a new haircut, close shave, and nose and ears hair-free – it didn't work though, did it? Sorry, Tony – just joking! I think you look absolutely gorgeous.

Anyway, as one in the know, having experienced the joys of marriage for the last two years, I would like to give Matt and Abi some genuine advice and perhaps words of comfort for the years to come: 'Marriage is a great university. It teaches you patience, consideration, understanding… and all sorts of rubbish you wouldn't need if you'd stayed single!' So let us raise our glasses once again – and I'm sure Mum will have no objections to that – and wish Matt and Abi everything that they could possibly desire for their future together.

Researching your speech

**Anyone who's landed the job of delivering
a speech will want to give it their best shot.**
You'll want it to be warm, witty and original. Even if
you don't know the couple very well (perhaps you're
standing in for someone) or aren't a born joker,
there are still plenty of ways you can make your
words really different and memorable. The key is
to pay attention to your material – and that means
research. Our handy guide offers tips and techniques
to help you beef up your speech.

Ask friends and family

It sounds obvious, but it's often overlooked – the best way to find out more about the subjects of your speech is to talk to their friends and relatives. Siblings, cousins, old school friends… each will have a different perspective on the stars of the day, and spending time chatting to them is sure to draw out half-forgotten anecdotal gems.

The best way to use this valuable resource is to get a group of friends and family together for a drink and a few reminiscences. While they sit there swapping stories, you may find the bulk of your speech will have been written for you by the end of the night. Bring along a tape recorder, too, so you can join in without worrying about taking notes.

Other sources

Once you've dredged the inner circle, you could extend your research to other areas of the past. Look through old photo albums, letters and cuttings – any of these might provide something funny to read out or hold up.

Track down people your subjects went to school with or worked with, such as former teachers and bosses. One best man – the groom's brother – went through his brother's old school books and found an essay, written at the age of 11, entitled 'The Girl I will Marry'. Naturally, his reading of this valuable document went down a treat on the big day.

Look to the stars

Another possible source of good material is horoscopes. Find out the star signs of your subjects, look into the associated characteristics and traits, and compare them with the person/people you're talking about. Much fun can be had, especially where the typical qualities don't match… or where the star sign's vices do!

For example, Aries has the following characteristics: courage, drive, heartiness, affability, talent and enterprise. Aries 'sins' may include naivety, ostentation, wilfulness, excess, sanctimony and domination. If your subject is a notorious coward who's famously careful with their money, you have the beginnings of a great gag.

Instead of star signs, you could use Chinese animal signs, which work in very much the same way.

Other ways to use horoscopes include finding books that discuss star-sign compatibility and/or quoting the horoscope of the day from a paper. Of course, it doesn't really have to be the actual day's column, and if you can create an ironic contrast between the theory and the reality – for instance, if your horoscope for the wedding day reads 'not much happening today' – you're bound to get a laugh.

For confetti.co.uk horoscopes check out: www.confetti.co.uk/speeches/p100

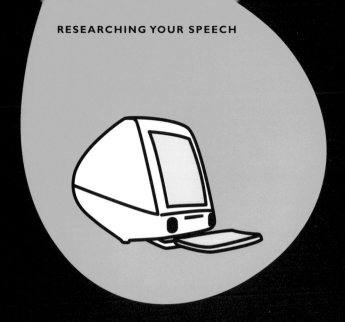

Consult the archives

Track down a newspaper(s) for the day your subject was
born and try to find an article that will fit whatever you are
writing about, or adapt a story to suit. You might be able to
find an old photograph that goes well with the article. Try
to make it look authentic and then get it blown up as big as
possible so it can be displayed while you're speaking. With
a little imagination, this could be visually very amusing.

Another way to get historical would be to refer to key
events that happened the day your subject was born/got
engaged/got married and so on. Again, this can be a good
source of humour. For example, 'John was born in the same
year that man first walked on the moon, which may not
seem particularly relevant until you've seen him trying to
dance when he's drunk.'

Totally topical

Look at current news stories you could put a twist on. Play around with the headlines and attach visuals to the article. Anyone with a PC and scanner can produce quite impressive-looking newspaper mock-ups to accompany their speech. The famous *Sun* headline 'Gotcha', for instance, could be used to accompany a picture of the happy couple on their engagement – even more apt (and comical) if the proposer had to ask several times!

What's in a name?

More material can be found in looking at the couple's names, and finding out what they really mean. If you're trying to make a sincere point about someone's qualities, the fact that their name comes from the Latin for 'strength' or 'love', and so on, can be a striking way of underlining the message. There is potential for comedy here, too, if there's an interesting contrast between the personality and the meaning, for example, if the groom's name is Daniel, which means 'God has chosen', and he is renowned for his atheist views!

Comparing the meanings of the names of both partners may provide some interesting material, too. 'Well, they say opposites attract…!' A dictionary of names and their meanings will help you with that one.

Celebrity help

Think of famous people with the same name as your bride
or groom and compare them to that celebrity in terms of
job, image, clothes, status, etc. Or does the bride or groom
admire a particular celebrity or person? Do they mirror
themselves on a famous person? What pop star did they
want to be as a child? Any comparisons or anecdotes on the
similarities (and differences!) between your subject and their
idol can be a good source of fun, too.

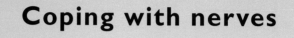

Coping with nerves

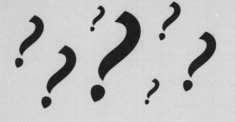

So you're making a speech at the wedding?
What's that? You've never made a speech before?
And there'll be how many people there? Over 100!
Wow! You must be terrified.

Relax. What follows is a user-friendly guide
to public speaking, covering everything from
preparation to delivery, that'll help you confront
your fears and have a really good time up there.

One of the best things about wedding speeches is that, from the moment you stand up to the moment you sit down, the entire audience is totally for you. The very reason you're standing up is because you are intimately connected with the people beside you – and so is the audience. All of which means that whatever you say will be listened to and respected. Not only that, but guests listening to speeches badly want to laugh because it breaks the tension and because they want to let you know they're with you. So, even a vague attempt at a gag will be warmly and hungrily received.

First things first

As you prepare yourself for the ordeal ahead, it's a good idea to think about why you've chosen to put yourself through it in the first place. The answer: because you care about the people for whom you're making the speech. You're doing it to make your friends and family happy. Bearing this in mind will help you make your speech personal, interesting, endearing and, often unintentionally, funny.

Thinking ahead

In most cases, you'll know a few months in advance that you'll have to make a speech, but even a few days' notice is more than enough time to consider, research and write it, provided you put your mind to it. Whatever time you have:

- Give your speech your undivided attention.
- Don't put it off until the night before the wedding.
- Sit down and write out ideas. The very act of doing this will spark other ideas.
- Play with your material. Get ten stories down on paper and pick the best three.
- Trim away waffle and repetition, then write out clearly what you have left.
- Keep it reasonably short – aim for three to five minutes.
- Remember the basic message of your speech, which is 'good luck and all the best'. Furnish with true stories. (Don't worry, they'll be funny – the truth always is.)

Putting it all together

The biggest aid to overcoming nerves when speaking in public is to be confident that you're well prepared, so:

- Write out your speech clearly and concisely in **BIG BOLD CAPITALS**. Keep the sentences short and clear.
- Make sure you have a definite beginning ('Ladies and gentlemen...'); a middle (a set list of stories and topics in a clear and logical order); and an end (your final words leading up to the toast).

Practice makes perfect

The more you practise delivering your speech, the less nervous you will be. Practise the pauses and the intonation of your voice. Practise your anecdotes, along with any impersonations you're planning. And remember: by showing that you've put even a little thought and effort into what you're saying, all manner of sins will be forgiven.

Recite your speech in the shower, in the car, on the bus, on the loo. Know it inside and out. Okay, it's a hassle, but on the day, your nerves will thank you big time. Why? Because instead of fretting about the audience/your appearance/your flies, you'll simply focus on what you're going to say. And that'll be easy, because you've said it at least 500 times a week for the last month!

At the reception

So, you're sitting at the top table with an hour till you speak. What should you do? Enjoy yourself – you've done all the hard work. Eat. Loosen your shoulders. Savour the occasion. Listen to the other speakers.

Remember that the celebrations are not about you – you're just a small part of a bigger deal. Remember, too, that what you're about to do is a service to others – not a court or a stage where the audience is your judge and jury. And also remember that it's a happy occasion, and your few words will simply add to it.

Allow yourself one drink, but make that the limit. Your adrenaline is all the booze you'll need. Have a drink as a reward *afterwards*. For now, having a clear head will keep you at your best.

Ten tips for a top performance

1. Don't let nerves stop you eating before your speech. Food really helps the nerves and provides a big energy hit. Many performers swear by this trick.

2. Remember to breathe – deeply and rhythmically. It pumps oxygen into your blood and keeps the brain alert.

3. Imagine it's over. This is a very popular NLP (neurolinguistic programming) technique. Before you stand up, visualize the end result, with you feeling elated and relieved and everyone else around you smiling and clapping. Thinking how great you'll feel will relax you in the present moment.

4. Have a laugh. Just before you stand up, think of a funny story or event that really tickles you, and let yourself laugh at it – even just a little. It will loosen you up and feed a sense of fun and enjoyment.

5. Smile! Be welcoming and warm. It sets the tone straight away and people will warm to you without knowing why.

6. Relax. It's your time, so take it. Everyone will listen to what you have to say because they want to. The speeches are always fun. Remember this and you'll deliver your words with confidence and ease.

7. Make eye contact with the audience. Look around you. The trick is to imagine that you're simply chatting to everyone there.

8. Speak slowly and clearly. Many speeches get the response, 'It was good, but I couldn't make out half of it.' Bearing this in mind will prevent you from jabbering.

9. Forget yourself. Take the weight off your ego by reflecting that the wedding is about other people, not you. Try not to take yourself too seriously – if people shout out heckles, go with it.

10. Enjoy yourself. Your life doesn't depend on your speech. You're not getting paid and it will be over in a few hundred seconds. Just give it your best shot.

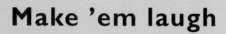

Make 'em laugh

Yikes! It's speech time and – groom, best man, father of the bride, even bride – it's you up next. You know what you're going to say, but will it be funny?

First of all relax. You're planning a wedding speech, not a slot as a stand-up comedian. Everyone will be on your side and ready to laugh at even the slightest attempt at humour. If you're planning to deliver your speech after the meal, then most of the guests will have had at least a glass or two of wine, so they'll be relaxed and in the mood for a laugh.

Don't feel that you have to fill your speech with witty one-liners – a few jokes spread judiciously through your speech will be more than enough. But whether you're aiming for a few wry smiles or side-splitting laughter, just be yourself because, after all, it's the real you that everyone wants to hear from.

Suitable material

Emotions run high at weddings, so steer clear of material
that could unwittingly cause offence. Avoid anything gross,
smutty or visually disturbing, as well as mean-spirited gags
at the expense of women drivers, mothers-in-law, and so on.
Use safe, gentle humour, appropriate to the situation and *all*
the wedding guests – including children, older people and
maiden aunts. 'In' jokes are always good at weddings, but
be careful not to reveal any incriminating secrets. Start by
making an instant connection through something that
everyone has seen that day: 'I think we all agree the bride
looks wonderful. That dress! Not like a wedding I was at
recently, where the bride and the wedding cake were
dressed exactly the same…' This way, no one present – or
even real – has to be the butt of the joke.

Telling a gag

A good joke can be ruined by poor delivery. No one will
laugh at something they can't hear, so speak clearly and don't
gabble. If the joke fails, then make the failure the joke. Comics
often use staple rescue lines such as, 'Only me on that one
then,' or, glancing around at an imaginary assistant, 'Start the
car!' Or try something like, 'I was running that gag in for
another best man/father of the bride. I'll tell him to bin it.'

Props

Well-chosen physical gags can work wonders. At one wedding, a best man known for his emotional outbursts threw out packs of paper tissues to everyone in preparation. (Sure enough, he was crying five minutes later – so they all got thrown back!) At another, a best man discovered the groom's secret plan to ride to the top table astride his beloved Harley Davidson. He retaliated by wheeling in behind him on a rickety trike!

Finally...

Keep your speech short. Less is definitely more – and brevity is most definitely the soul of wit. Don't try too hard – a heartfelt, affectionate speech that raise smiles is much better than an OTT, hammy performance that causes the entire wedding party to cringe.

If you need a little extra inspiration, here are a few jokes and words of wisdom to lighten up your speech!

One man says to another, 'I never knew the meaning of happiness until I got married, but by then it was too late!'

'I have the perfect husband,' says one woman to another.
'What makes you say that?' says her friend.
'He remembers my birthday, but forgets my age!'

A man who gives in when he is wrong is a wise man. A man who gives in when he is right is married.

A policeman who arrested a woman for murder asked, 'Why did you shoot your husband with a bow and arrow?'
She replied, 'I didn't want to wake the children.'

'Why did you make woman so beautiful?' a man asked God.
God replied, 'So you would love her.'
'Why did you give woman amazing culinary skills?' the man asked.
God said, 'So you would love her.'
'Why, if you wanted man to love woman, why did you make woman so stupid?' asked the man.
And God replied 'So she would love you.'

'I had such an argument with my wife last night, Shaun, but we sorted it out eventually,' Bill says, one lunchtime in the pub. 'She wanted to go to bingo and I wanted to go to the cinema.'
'So how was the bingo?' replies Shaun with a grin.

Day and night, a woman sits by her husband's hospital bedside as he lies in a coma for months on end. Finally, he wakes up. 'You have stood by me through thick and thin. When I lost my job, when we lost the house, you were there by my side. When our son died and the dog ran off, you supported me. When my business crumbled and then again when I got shot. And now my health is failing and you are still beside me, helping me through it all. It's really starting to annoy me – I was fine before I married you!'

A father and son are walking through a chemists, and the son picks up a packet of condoms and says, 'Dad, what are these?' So the father explains.
The son then asks, 'Why do they come in packs of three, six and twelve?'
His father replies, 'The packs of three are for teenage boys. They use one on Friday night, one on Saturday night and one on Sunday night. The packs of six are for twentysomethings. They use two on Friday, two on Saturday and two on Sunday. The twelve packs are for married men. They use one in January, one in February...'

Satan appears to a congregation before mass is due to start. Once everyone realizes that Beelzebub is standing before them, they all get up and run, except one man. He just sits there staring at Evil personified. The Devil is slightly perplexed by this as it has been many centuries since someone has had the courage to be seated in his presence. So, he goes to the man and asks, 'Why are you not scared of me as the rest of your people are?' The man replies, 'I've been married to your sister for 25 years.'

Why is it more advantageous for a woman to be pretty than for her to be intelligent?
Because men have better vision than they do minds.

A little boy says to his dad, 'In some parts of the world, a man doesn't know his wife before he marries her. Is that true?'
'That's the case the world over,' replies his father.

A husband is living proof that a wife can take a joke.'
(Helen Rowland)

Long engagements give people the opportunity of finding out each other's character before marriage, which is never advisable.
(Oscar Wilde)

My wife and I were happy for 20 years. And then we met.'
(Rodney Dangerfield)

'Never go to bed on an argument, stay up and fight.'
(Phyllis Diller)

A man is contemplating sunbathing nude in his back garden and asks his wife for her opinion. 'The neighbours will think I married you for your money,' came her reply.

Groom to bride: 'For your honeymoon, I'm going to take you somewhere hot and steamy you've never been!'
Bride: 'Where's that?'
Groom: 'The kitchen!'

'Do you realize what you did?' a woman asked her husband.
'No, but I am sorry for it,' he replied.

Wife: 'It took me until after we were married to discover how
stupid you are.'
Husband: 'You should have realized that the moment I proposed.'

'My advice to you,' a mother told her daughter, 'is that if he's
giving you all that you ask for, then you aren't asking for enough.'

'Why is your belly so big?' the young daughter asked her mother.
'There's a baby in there,' the mother explained.
'How did it get in there?'
'Your father gave it to me.'
So off went the little girl to her father.
'Dad... you know you gave Mum that baby?'
'Yes?' said her father.
'She's swallowed it.'

'My wife and I have the greatest arrangement,' one man said to
the other. 'There is nothing one of us wouldn't do for the other.
That's how we like it, never doing anything for each other!'

'You come home from work every day and I ask you how it went,'
Mrs McBrien said to her husband. 'And every day I listen to all
that happened. You never ask me how my day went. You never
take any interest in my day.'
'So, how was your day?' Mr McBrien asked with a sigh.
'Don't ask!' she said, turning away.

Speech games

**There are several 'games' you can play to
enliven even the most exciting wedding,** and
they are a great addition for those who want to bring
something different to their speeches. Here, we've
included some of the best: The key game, This is your
life, Limericks, Sing to me! and Sweepstake.

The key game

This is one of the best 'speech' games we know. Bewildered?
Let us explain:

- Pass a note around the female guests or speak to them beforehand about their role in the game. You can loiter outside the ladies' toilets and catch them as they come out, but try not to look too obvious or someone might twig that you're up to something – or talk!

- During the speech, ask any of the groom's ex-girlfriends to return his house/flat keys, and, you've guessed it, *all* the female guests, from 89-year-old Aunt Flo to little Alice, the three-year-old flower girl, will come up to the well-placed bowl (arrange for an empty bowl to be placed on a side table where everyone can see it) and put a set of keys in it. Guaranteed to bring the house down!

- The key game can also be adapted for a father of the bride's speech, asking all those who stayed over at the family home in the past to return the spare keys. This time, involve all the male guests in the scheming.

This is your life

Some people go to the trouble of making a book that commemorates important moments in the bride or groom's life. Include things like:

- A sample of their handwriting at primary school (ask their parents for help if you don't have anything that old).
- The worst photos imaginable.
- Details of an early date with the groom or bride.
- Any newspaper cuttings from their life, including childhood sporting achievements or local theatre appearances.
- Although creating the book does take time, our brides have told us how much the gesture was appreciated and how it kept the entire wedding party entertained for ages, long after the carefully written speeches were given!
- You may prefer to show a home video or blow up old photographs instead.

Limericks

A quick way of adding a little audience anticipation:

- Put a note on each table asking guests to come up with a short poem or a couple of lines about the bride and groom.
- Read out the best ones during the speech or, if you make it clear that they must not be offensive, ask each table to read their best efforts out in turn.
- You might like to play safe and make up the first two lines of a limerick yourself, then ask guests to finish it off with the last two lines. For example:

*There was **a young/an old** woman from*
*[**place where lives/born/works**]*
*Who fell in love with **[name/career]**...*

We stood up to toast the couple
When the bride got up to say...

*The **vicar/registrar/photographer***
*looked at the **bride/groom***
*And scratched **his/her** nose in disgust*

*There was a young man from **[Uni/place***
where he works/was born/lives]
Who decided he wanted to marry...

Sing to me!

One for the more artistic and less self-conscious!

- The bride and groom compile a list of words that describe each guest on a table.
- These lists are placed under the table centrepieces.
- Each table has to compose a poem or song using all of these words and then stand up and perform it.

Sweepstake

Before the speeches start, have the ushers tour the reception asking guests to bet on the length of time they estimate all the speeches will last.

- Write down each person and their predictions.
- Charge 10p–£1 a go.
- Make sure your usher has a stopwatch running and can take verbal abuse from the losers!
- The person closest to the exact time wins the total amount. Alternatively, you could use the game as a way of raising money for charity or even starting a slush fund for the bride and groom.

Launched in February 1999, confetti.co.uk is the UK's leading wedding website, helping over 100,000 brides, grooms and guests every month.

Free and easy to use, confetti.co.uk is packed full of ideas and advice to help organize every stage of your wedding. At confetti.co.uk, you can choose from hundreds of beautiful wedding dresses; investigate our list of more than 3,000 wedding and reception venues; plan your wedding; chat to other brides about their experiences; and ask for advice from Aunt Betti, our agony aunt. If your guests are online too, we will even help you set up a wedding website to share details and photos with your family and friends.

Confetti.co.uk also runs the UK's fastest growing wedding list service, offering unbeatable choice and convenience. To select your gifts you can either go online or order a copy of the confetti.co.uk gift book. Your guests can then order their gifts by phone from one of our wedding consultants or 24 hours a day on the internet.

If you want your reception to go with a bang, the wedding and party shop at confetti.co.uk stocks everything you need from streamers to candles and even disposable cameras. It's ideal for all your special occasions… not only weddings!

To find out more or to order your confetti.co.uk gift book or party brochure, visit www.confetti.co.uk, call 0870 840 6060, or e-mail us at info@confetti.co.uk